AnimalWays

Penguins

AnimalWays

Penguins

Rebecca Stefoff

Marshall Cavendish
Benchmark
New York

With thanks to Dr. Dan Wharton, director of the Central Park Wildlife Center, for his expert reading of this manuscript.

Marshall Cavendish Benchmark
99 White Plains Road
Tarrytown, NY 10591
www.marshallcavendish.us

Text copyright © 2005 by Rebecca Stefoff
Illustrations copyright © 2005 by Ka Botzis
Map by Carol Matsuyama
Map copyright © 2005 by Marshall Cavendish Corporation

All Internet sites were available and accurate when sent to press.

Library of Congress Cataloging-in-Publication Data

Stefoff, Rebecca, 1951-
Penguins / by Rebecca Stefoff.
p. cm. — (Animalways)
Summary: Discusses the evolution, biology, life cycle, and social and mating behavior of penguins.
Includes bibliographical references (p.   ) and index.
ISBN 0-7614-1743-5
1. Penguins—Juvenile literature. [1. Penguins.] I. Title. II. Series.

QL696.S473S724 2003
598.47--dc22
2003022113

Photo Research by Candlepants Incorporated

Cover Photo: Peter Arnold, Inc./Robert Angell

The photographs in this book are used by permission and through the courtesy of: *Peter Arnold, Inc.*/Kim Heacox, title page, 30; Kevin Schafer, 9, 33, 39, 42 (top), 49, 61, 65, 79; Martin Harvey, 13, 47, 72, 89, 103; Fritz Polking, 16, 23, 51, 78, 81; Roland Seitre/Bios, 32, 83; Gunter Ziesler, 34; Fred Bruemmer, 37, 50, 75, 101; Doug Cheesman, 40, 54 (bottom), 76; John Cancalosi, 42 (bottom), 44; Jochen Tack/Das Fotoarchiv, 54 (top), 93, 94; Alain Torterotot, 60; Tom Vezo, 63; Gunter Ziesler, 69; Thierry Thomas/BIOS, 82; Frederic Beauchene/BIOS, 85; Joel Bennett, back cover; *Art Archive*/Biblioteque des Artes Decorative/Paris/Dagli Orti, 12; *Photo Researchers, Inc.*/Andrew Syred, 19; G. I. Bernard P.R., 20; R. W. Hernandez, 85; *Minden Pictures*/ Frans Lanting, 98.

Printed in China

1 3 5 6 4 2

Contents

Animal Kingdom

CNIDARIANS

coral

ARTHROPODS
(animals with
jointed limbs and
external skeleton)

MOLLUSKS

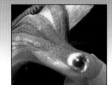

squid

CRUSTACEANS

crab

ARACHNIDS

spider

INSECTS

grasshopper

MYRIAPODS

centipede

CARNIVORES

lion

SEA MAMMALS

whale

PRIMATES

orangutan

HERBIVORES
(5 orders)

elephant

PHYLA

ANNELIDS

earthworm

CHORDATES
(animals with a dorsal nerve chord)

ECHINODERMS

starfish

SUB PHYLA

VERTEBRATES
(animals with a backbone)

CLASSES

FISH
fish

BIRDS
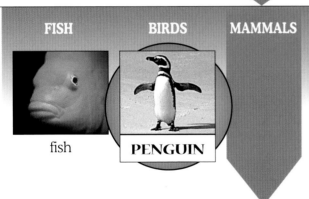
PENGUIN

MAMMALS

AMPHIBIANS

frog

REPTILES

snake

ORDERS

RODENTS

squirrel

INSECTIVORES

mole

MARSUPIALS

koala

SMALL MAMMALS
(several orders)

bat

1 Flightless Birds of the Southern Sea

In her book *Penguin Summer*, Eleanor Rice Pettingill wrote about her first glimpse of a beach alive with excited gentoo penguins. "Some were clustered in small groups," she wrote, "others were milling around, still others were trumpeting; a very few were motionless, merely watching. It looked as though the penguins were having a party."

The behavior of the black-and-white birds fascinated Pettingill. She described the antics that penguin-watchers find comical and appealing:

> *The birds in the small groups were clicking bills. . . . Two birds would walk up to each other, put their heads together as if exchanging secrets, then click their bills together faster and faster. They were joined by others until there*

KING PENGUINS ARE THE SECOND LARGEST PENGUINS. THEIR COLONIES ARE SCENES OF CONSTANT INTERACTION AMONG BIRDS, SOMETIMES SQUABBLING, SOMETIMES ENJOYING EACH OTHER'S COMPANY.

were six or eight in a circle, all leaning toward the center clicking bills madly. Then suddenly they all raised their heads and walked away, possibly to form other groups.

The more extroverted birds were trumpeting—a process that involved the whole penguin. A bird about to trumpet puffed itself full of air, held its head and bill straight up, and like a bellows emitted the air in a series of gusts that produced the most doleful braying sounds, quite inconsistent with the spirit of a beach party. Each trumpeter attracted other penguins, which gathered around it as if to marvel that so much noise could come from one of their number. We heard these noises at night . . . they were blood-curdling and fearful in the dark, but ridiculous in the sunshine.

Every so often a few penguins decided to go for a swim. They waded into the water up to their flippers, bent down slowly, and were away in a flash. From where we stood on the top of the cliff their black bodies showed up clearly against the sandy bottom and we were aware of a metamorphosis. The clumsy bird that ambled into the water was transformed into a sleek black torpedo, darting about with incredible speed. The flippers, once its wings, became propellers; its flat yellow feet acted as rudders. One group after another waddled into the water, shot straight out, circled several times, and returned to the beach. We admired their perfect streamlining and their festive air. They did not go into the water to feed or to bathe, but just to play, to enjoy being penguins.

Published in 1960, Pettingill's book told of a season spent with her ornithologist husband in the Falkland Islands, off the coast of South America in the South Atlantic Ocean, observing and filming king and Magellanic penguins. *Penguin Summer* was one of the first books to give the general public a close look at penguins and their lives, and it found many enthusiastic readers. In the passage quoted here and in other parts of the book, Pettingill pinpointed the things that many people love about penguins—their interactions with each other, the fact that they often seem to look like little people wearing black-and-white tuxedos, and the way their clumsy, waddling walk changes to smooth, efficient swimming as soon as they enter the water. All of those features are related to the biology and way of life of penguins. They interact with each other in a variety of ways because they are communal animals who live in groups. They resemble small people because they walk upright with their legs directly beneath them, rather than tilted forward, like other birds. The black-and-white coloring that reminds many observers of fancy clothing is a form of camouflage that protects penguins from predators. Penguins have a clumsy and comical-looking walk because their legs are very short, but they swim with great elegance because water is their natural element, the place where they find food and spend much of their time.

Much more is known about penguins today than in 1953, when Pettingill and her husband made their pioneering study of Falklands penguins. The birds are as appealing as ever—penguins are always one of a zoo's most popular exhibits. Yet in recent years scientists have gained new knowledge and insights into how these remarkable birds evolved, how they live, and how their survival depends upon the survival of ecosystems in the ocean and on land. The complex picture of penguins that emerges from these studies is even more fascinating than the birds' adorable antics.

MANY OCEAN-GOING BIRDS SHARE THE PENGUIN'S BLACK-ON-TOP, WHITE-BELOW
COLORING AND STREAMLINED SHAPE. THERE ARE ALSO SIMILARITIES IN THE HABITATS
AND BEHAVIOR OF THESE BIRDS: (FRONT, LEFT TO RIGHT) A GREAT AUK, A PENGUIN, A
GUILLEMOT, AND A LOON, AND (REAR, LEFT TO RIGHT) A CORMORANT, A PUFFIN, AND
A SHEARWATER.

What Is a Penguin?

Europeans did not see penguins until they began venturing into
waters far from their own shores. The first Europeans to see penguins may have been Portuguese navigator Bartolomeu Dias
and his men, who sailed around the southern tip of Africa in

1488. The first to make a record of penguins was Alvero Vello, who sailed around Africa in 1497 with Vasco da Gama, another Portuguese navigator. Vello wrote that on an island off the South African coast there were "birds as big as ducks, but they cannot fly because they have no feathers on their wings. These birds of whom we killed as many as we choose . . . bray like asses." The African penguins native to those waters belong to a group

AFRICAN PENGUINS—SOMETIMES CALLED BLACK-FOOTED OR JACKASS PENGUINS—BELONG TO A GROUP OF SPECIES KNOWN AS THE BANDED PENGUINS BECAUSE OF THEIR CHEST STRIPES. THE BARE SKIN AROUND THE EYES OF THE AFRICAN PENGUIN LETS EXCESS HEAT ESCAPE, AND ITS RED COLOR BRIGHTENS DURING THEIR MATING SEASON.

sometimes called the jackass penguins because the noises they make resemble the braying of donkeys or jackasses.

In 1519 and 1520, another Portuguese explorer, Ferdinand Magellan, led the first European expedition that sailed along the Atlantic coast of South America to the southern tip of that continent. He and his men saw the South American penguins that are today called Magellanic penguins in his honor. However, neither Vello nor Magellan called the strange new flightless birds they saw in the southern oceans penguins. In their day, the name penguin referred to a different bird entirely.

To mariners and fishermen in the North Atlantic Ocean, penguin was one of several names for a large, flightless swimming bird called the great auk. Language historians have several ideas about the origins and meaning of the name penguin. Some think that it came from the Welsh words *pen gwynn*, which mean "white head," because seamen identified the great auk by a distinctive white patch on its black head. Others think that it came from *penguis*, a form of the Latin word for "fat," or that it was a version of the English words "pin wing." Whatever the origin of the word, the great auk was given the scientific name *Pinguinis impennis*. The great auk became extinct in 1844, when hunters captured the last two auks and their egg on Funk Island, off the coast of Iceland. By that time, however, seafaring Europeans had given the name "penguin" to birds in the Southern Hemisphere. And although the original penguin is long gone, the southern birds are still called penguins.

At first, Europeans weren't sure that the southern penguins *were* birds. Some thought that they were fish because they swam so well. Others thought that they were marine mammals, similar to seals, because their tiny, smooth feathers looked like fur. But by the middle of the sixteenth century, penguins had been recognized as birds. Another two hundred years passed before eighteenth-century European scientists began writing and publishing zoological descriptions of penguins, as well as identifying and naming the various penguin species.

At Home at the Bottom of the World

Penguins live only in the Southern Hemisphere. Their natural habitats fall into three general groups. One group includes parts of the coastlines and some of the coastal islands of South America, Africa, Australia, New Zealand, and Antarctica. Another group consists of the subantarctic islands, small specks of land scattered through the southern Atlantic, Indian, and Pacific Oceans, not far north of the Antarctic Circle. The third group is the Galápagos Islands, on the equator in the Pacific Ocean. Much farther north than the other penguin habitats, the Galápagos Islands are home to a single species of penguin.

In all of these places, penguins are found in or near the water. They are pelagic birds, which means that they spend a large part of their lives in the open sea. Says science writer James Gorman, author of *The Total Penguin*, "The real territory of penguins is not the Antarctic or South American coast, or the windy islands of the Southern Ocean, but the ocean itself."

Penguins have become symbols of Antarctica and of polar cold. In cartoons and advertisements, they perch on icebergs or toddle past the South Pole. In reality, no penguins live at the South Pole, which is far inland. Only a few of the seventeen species live in Antarctica, and several species live in tropical climates. A great number of penguins, however, *do* live in extremely cold conditions, and all penguin habitats share one feature: cool water.

Penguins live where ocean temperatures are cooler than 68 degrees Fahrenheit (20 degrees Celsius). Some species live in waters that are *much* cooler. Emperor penguins, for example, inhabit Antarctic waters having an average temperature of about 32 degrees Fahrenheit (0 degrees Celsius)—temperatures low enough to freeze freshwater, although seawater freezes at lower temperatures because of its salt content. Most penguin

species live in waters that are milder, although still quite cold. The Galápagos and Humboldt penguins, the equatorial species, are the exceptions. They are at home in waters with an average temperature of about 73 degrees Fahrenheit (23 degrees Celsius), warmer than the habitats of all other penguins but unusually cold for equatorial seas. Humboldt penguins survive on the coast of the Peruvian desert because of the Humboldt Current, a stream of cold water that flows northward from the Antarctic to the Equator along the west coast of South America, lowering the water temperature. Galápagos penguins owe their survival to the Cromwell Current, a deep flow of cold water that rises to the surface when it strikes the submerged bases of the Galápagos Islands.

The chilling effect of the Humboldt and Cromwell Currents is just part of a complex system of water movements that defines the world of penguins. The system begins at the bottom of the world, in Antarctica. In winter, strong winds blow northward from

BORN IN THE COLDEST PLACE ON EARTH, EMPEROR PENGUIN CHICKS NEED THICK COATS OF VERY WARM FEATHERS TO SURVIVE. THESE YOUNG PENGUINS WILL NOT BE ABLE TO SWIM, HOWEVER, UNTIL THEY HAVE RECEIVED THEIR FIRST WATERPROOF FEATHERS.

the center of the continent, pushing cold water away from the coast. In summer, ice melts to become cold water that also flows north, away from the continent. Winter and summer, Antarctica is the source of a steady northward flow of very cold water. Far from the Antarctic coast, at about 50 degrees of latitude south of the Equator, this northward flow meets the West Wind Drift, one of the strongest currents in the world's oceans. Pushed by constant westerly winds, the West Wind Drift flows from east to west around the entire planet between 40 and 50 degrees south. The winds—and the massive waves and storms they create—have earned these southerly latitudes respectful nicknames among sailors: the Roaring Forties and the Furious Fifties.

The zone where the cold, north-flowing Antarctic waters meet the West Wind Drift is called the Antarctic Convergence. A convergence is a coming-together, but the two masses of seawater that meet at the Antarctic Convergence do not blend. Instead, when the Antarctic waters collide with the slightly warmer waters of the West Wind Drift, they sink and turn southward, flowing back toward Antarctica, deep in the ocean. When these low, southbound currents hit the Antarctic coast they rise to the surface, carrying enormous amounts of nutrients up from the ocean floor. This rich upwelling makes the ocean waters around Antarctica teem with life. The nutrients are bits of organic matter from animal waste and from countless dead plants and animals. They support vast quantities of tiny organisms called plankton. The plankton, in turn, feed millions upon millions of small, shrimplike animals called krill. And the krill provide food for fish, squid, whales, and penguins.

Meanwhile, the West Wind Drift continues its steady, round-the-world flow. Because its waters are so stormy, nutrients do not sink to the ocean bottom. Instead, they hang in the water, which also contains much oxygen because it is stirred up by

MARINE ZOOPLANKTON ARE TINY ANIMALS THAT THRIVE IN THE COLD WATERS OF THE SOUTHERN OCEANS. TOGETHER WITH TINY PLANTS CALLED PHOTOPLANKTON, THEY FORM THE BASIS OF THE OCEAN'S FOOD CHAIN. PENGUINS DON'T EAT PLANKTON, BUT THEY DO EAT THE SHRIMP, CRABS, AND FISH THAT FEED ON IT.

winds and waves. This combination of oxygen and nutrients means that the West Wind Drift, like the upwelling along the Antarctic coast, is rich in life. And where this broad current strikes the western shores of land masses, parts of it spin off to form smaller currents along the coastlines. The Humboldt is one such current. The Benguela Current, which flows north along

THIS PICTURE OF A GREAT AUK WAS PUBLISHED IN 1893, ALMOST FIFTY YEARS AFTER
HUNTERS KILLED THE LAST OF THE SPECIES. THE GREAT AUK WAS THE FIRST BIRD TO
BE CALLED A PENGUIN, ALTHOUGH IT WAS NOT PART OF THE BIRD FAMILY NOW
KNOWN BY THAT NAME.

the coast of southwestern Africa, is another. A third current spins off to flow up the coast of New Zealand. All of these currents carry nutrient-rich cold water north, extending the range of animals that flourish in the chilly southern sea. Among the animals that have evolved to live in such waters are the penguins.

2 Penguins, Yesterday and Today

Penguins have been around for about fifty-five million years. Scientists working to piece together their history are especially curious about several things: When and where did penguins first appear? How did they lose the ability to fly? How are the modern species of penguins related to the extinct penguins known from fossils? And what other living birds are penguins' closest relatives?

Origins

No fossils of penguins have ever been found in the Northern Hemisphere. Paleontologists, scientists who study the remains of ancient and extinct creatures, think that penguins originated in the Southern Hemisphere and have always lived only in that part of the world. Scientists are not certain *where* penguins originated, but some think that New Zealand is a good possibility. Many fossils of ancient penguins have been found in New

EMPEROR PENGUINS SHUFFLE THROUGH A SNOWSTORM ON THE DAWSON-LAMBTON GLACIER IN ANTARCTICA. EMPERORS LIVE IN CONDITIONS SO SEVERE THAT A WRITER CALLED HIS 1911 EXPEDITION TO ONE OF THEIR COLONIES *THE WORST JOURNEY IN THE WORLD*.

Zealand, and today New Zealand and its neighboring small islands have five species of penguins. Ornithologist Roger Tory Peterson, who studied penguins and was so interested in them that his nickname was King Penguin, wrote in his book *Penguins* that the seas around New Zealand, rich in marine life, "may well have been the theater of evolution that witnessed the emergence of the penguins as a unique family of flightless birds."

Until the middle of the twentieth century, scientists thought that penguins had evolved from ancestors that had always been flightless. Some suggested that penguins were survivors from an early stage in the evolution of birds, a branch of the bird family that had never achieved the power of flight. Today, however, scientists know from careful study of the bodies of living penguins and fossils of extinct ones that penguins are descended from birds that flew. They evolved into flightless birds—or at least into birds possessing the ability for a different kind of flight. Wrote William Ashworth in *Penguins, Puffins, and Auks*, "Penguins' wings are still wings, and they are still used for flight. The difference between them and the wings of other birds is that they are designed to fly through the water."

Paleontologists rely on fossils to answer questions about how plants and animals evolved over millions of years. Unfortunately, the fossil record for penguins is far from complete. Most penguin fossils are not complete, or even partial, skeletons. Instead, they are skull parts and individual bones from the legs and from the wings, or flippers. By comparing these fragments with the same pieces from existing species of penguins, scientists can estimate the size of the extinct species. They can also determine whether the extinct penguins belonged to the same subgroups as modern penguins or to different subgroups.

Penguin fossils have been found in many places where penguins live today, but none have been found in places where

Where Penguins Live

AFRICA

Tristan Da Cunha
Gough I.
Cape of
Good Hope

"Roaring Forties"

ATLANTIC OCEAN

GREENWICH MERIDIAN

Bouvet I.

Prince Edward Is.

"Furious Fifties"

South Georgia

South
Sandwich Is.

Crozet Is.

ANTARCTIC CIRCLE

Falkland Is.

South Orkney Is.

Kerguelen Is.

South Shetland Is.

Tierra
Del Fuego
Cape Horn

*WEDDELL
SEA*

Heard I.

*SOUTH
AMERICA*

Antarctic
Peninsula

*INDIAN
OCEAN*

Galapagos Is.

ANTARCTICA

+ *SOUTH POLE*

Peter Is.

*PACIFIC
OCEAN*

ROSS SEA

ANTARCTIC CONVERGENCE

ANTARCTIC CIRCLE

Balleny Is.

Galápagos Is.

Fernandina
Isabella
S. Cruz

Galápagos Is.

*SOUTH
AMERICA*

*PACIFIC
OCEAN*

*ATLANTIC
OCEAN*

DATE LINE

Macquarie Is.

Campbell I.
Auckland Is.

TASMANIA

*PACIFIC
OCEAN*

The Snares

Antipodes Is.
Bounty Is.

South
Island

AUSTRALIA

Chatham Is.

NEW ZEALAND

North
Island

modern penguins *don't* live. This means that penguins have probably occupied the same range, or part of the world, throughout their history. They probably always lived in or near bodies of water. Most experts believe that penguins descended from birds that both flew in the air and swam in the sea, as some kinds of birds do today. Some of these ancestral birds developed features such as stiffer wings and heavier bones that made them better swimmers but less efficient flyers. Over time they lost the ability to fly, but they became superb swimmers. These were the first penguins. No fossils have yet been found of birds at an evolutionary stage between flightless penguins and their flying ancestors. For this reason, some paleontologists think that penguins evolved fairly quickly. The first penguins may have evolved from flying birds in just a million years or so—a short time in terms of the long history of evolution.

Penguins evolved into a variety of species. Scientists have identified several dozen extinct species from fossil remains, and some believe that many unknown species remain to be discovered. About a dozen of the extinct species appear to have been larger than any penguins alive today. One of the earliest known species, called *Anthropornis nodernskjoeldi*, lived anywhere from thirty-seven to forty-five million years ago and was between 64 and 72 inches (160 and 180 centimeters) tall. With a standing height of approximately 5.5 feet (1.7 meters), it was taller than many modern humans. It was also much taller than the biggest modern penguin, the emperor, which has an average standing height of about 35 inches (90 cm). Another penguin from the same time period, *Pachydyptes ponderosus*, was slightly shorter but probably weighed between 220 and 240 pounds (99 and 108 kilograms). Paleontologist George Gaylord Simpson, who surveyed the evolution of penguins in *Penguins: Past and Present, Here and There* (1976), noted that although *Pachydyptes*

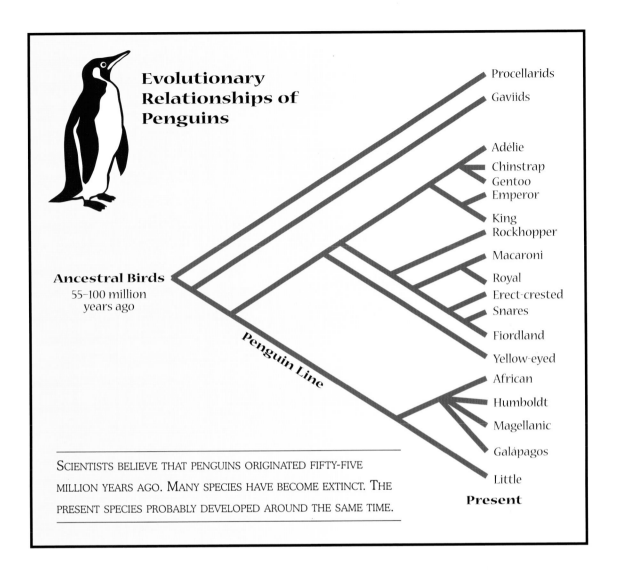

Evolutionary Relationships of Penguins

Procellarids
Gaviids
Adélie
Chinstrap
Gentoo
Emperor
King
Rockhopper
Macaroni
Royal
Erect-crested
Snares
Fiordland
Yellow-eyed
African
Humboldt
Magellanic
Galápagos
Little
Present

Ancestral Birds
55–100 million years ago

Penguin Line

SCIENTISTS BELIEVE THAT PENGUINS ORIGINATED FIFTY-FIVE MILLION YEARS AGO. MANY SPECIES HAVE BECOME EXTINCT. THE PRESENT SPECIES PROBABLY DEVELOPED AROUND THE SAME TIME.

ponderosus was not tall enough for basketball, it would have been sturdy enough to play football.

Of the extinct penguin species that scientists have identified, only two are closely related to modern penguins. *Aptenodytes ridgeni* lived in New Zealand between 3.5 and 5.5 million years ago. Scientists have placed this extinct penguin in the same genus—the category that includes related species—as the modern emperor and king penguins, and it was probably about the size of an emperor. Somewhat smaller was *Pygoscelis tyreei*, which lived around the same time, also in New Zealand. It belongs to the same genus as the modern Adélie, chinstrap, and gentoo penguins. Paleontologists and ornithologists hope that future fossil finds will tell us more about how these birds are related to today's penguins and about penguin origins and evolution in general.

Scientific Classification

Scientists use a system called taxonomy to classify and name plants and animals. Taxonomy is a series of categories, or levels, each more specific and narrowly defined than the last. The largest category is the kingdom, and the smallest is the species, which includes just one kind of organism.

The taxonomy of penguins is the same as that of other birds through the first few levels of classification. At the level called the order, though, penguins separate from the other birds. Here is the scientific classification of penguins, from kingdom to species.

Kingdom: Animalia (animals)
Phylum: Chordata (animals with spinal chords)
Subphylum: Vertebrata (animals with backbones around their spinal chords)
Class: Aves (birds)
Subclass: Neornithes (birds with no teeth)
Superorder: Neognathes (birds with keels, bony formations in their chests to which wing muscles are attached)
Order: Sphenisciformes (flightless swimming birds)
Family: Spheniscidae (penguins, the only family in the Sphenisciformes order)
Genus: six genera of living penguins
Species: seventeen species of living penguins

The number of penguin species existing today varies from sixteen to eighteen, depending upon the scientist doing the classifying. Most classifications, however, recognize seventeen species of penguins in six genera. All penguins have dark backs and light fronts, but each species has distinctive details of coloration and markings on the head and neck.

Aptenodytes Genus. The genus *Aptenodytes* contains two species of penguins, the emperor and the king. These are the largest modern penguins. Both species are cold-water dwellers, preferring water temperatures not much higher than 45 degrees Fahrenheit (7.2 degrees Celsius). The genus name, Latin for "featherless divers," is only half accurate. Although the emperor and king penguins are excellent divers, they are thoroughly covered with feathers.

Emperor penguins, whose scientific name is *Aptenodytes forsteri*, are the largest penguins, with an average height of 35 inches (90 cm) and an average weight of 66 pounds (30 kg). Some emperors weigh as much as 90 pounds (41 kg). Their backs are blue-gray rather than black, and their fronts have a yellowish tint. Emperors also have distinctive yellow patches on the sides of their heads.

Emperor penguins are truly Antarctic birds. They spend much of their lives swimming and hunting in the Antarctic Ocean. Emperors feed on squid, fish, and crabs. When they come ashore, it is to breed and raise their chicks in forty or so large communities called colonies. Several of these colonies are located on small islands near the coast of Antarctica, but most colonies form on sea ice, which exists only during the Antarctic winter (May into September), when the sea near Antarctica freezes. Emperors are the only penguins that breed during the

KING PENGUINS ARE A POPULAR ATTRACTION IN MANY ZOOS AROUND THE WORLD. AT THE EDINBURGH ZOO IN SCOTLAND, FOR EXAMPLE, VISITORS CAN WATCH THEM TAKING A DAILY STROLL AROUND THE ZOO GROUNDS. THESE KINGS, HOWEVER, ARE AT HOME ON THE FALKLAND ISLANDS.

winter. They raise their young chicks in the midst of some of the harshest weather on the planet.

King penguins, *Aptenodytes patagonica*, are a bit shorter and significantly less stout than emperors. A king's average height is 32 inches (81 cm), and its average weight is 33 pounds (15 kg). Kings have blue-gray backs and white fronts with yellow tints under their chins. Their most distinctive feature is bright gold-orange patches on the sides of their heads. King penguins inhabit a milder climate than emperors do. They live on sub-antarctic islands, including the Falklands, Crozets, Kerguelens, South Georgia, and Macquarie. Kings do not swim as far or dive as deep as emperors. They feed on smaller fish, shrimp, and squid.

Pygoscelis Genus. The *Pygoscelis* genus includes three species that scientists call the pygoscelid penguins: Adélies, chinstraps, and gentoos. *Pygoscelid* is sometimes translated as "rump-legged" and sometimes as "brush-tailed." Either way, the name refers to the stiff tails of all three species, which drag on the ground and look almost like a third leg.

Adélie penguins, or *Pygoscelis adeliae*, are the only penguins other than emperors that live in Antarctica. Their colonies are found on rocky stretches of the Antarctic coastline as well as on the South Shetland, the South Sandwich, and other sub-antarctic islands. Adélies eat krill and small fish. They average 29 inches (73 cm) in height and 11 pounds (5 kg) in weight. The Adélies' most distinctive marking is the white ring around each eye. Their name comes from Adélie Land, a part of the Antarctic coast that French explorer Jules-Sébastien-César Dumont d'Urville named for his wife in 1840. Scientists in his expedition applied the name to the penguins they saw in the region.

The chinstrap penguin has the scientific name *Pygoscelis Antarctica*, which is geographically off base. The chinstrap does not live in Antarctica. Instead, it inhabits subantarctic islands south of South America and along the Antarctic Peninsula—including Elephant Island, where members of Ernest Shackleton's shipwrecked 1915 Antarctic expedition survived for months by dining on the local chinstrap colony. Chinstraps eat

THE FLESHY SPIKES OR BARBS IN THIS ADÉLIE PENGUIN'S MOUTH POINT DOWN TOWARD ITS STOMACH, PREVENTING THE FISH IT CATCHES FROM ESCAPING. ALL PENGUIN SPECIES HAVE THESE USEFUL BARBS.

krill and small fish. They stand 29 inches (73 cm) tall and weigh about 10 pounds (4.5 kg). Their common name comes from their most recognizable marking: a white face with a narrow black band that runs from side to side under their eyes and bill. That dark band reminded nineteenth-century explorers of the chin strap on the helmets of British policemen.

The third pygoscelid penguin is the gentoo, *Pygoscelis papua*. Like the chinstrap, the gentoo has a scientific name that is geographically inaccurate—dramatically so. Papua is part of New Guinea, a tropical island north of Australia, thousands of miles from any penguins. John Forster, a scientist who

CHINSTRAP PENGUINS LIVE ON ISLANDS NEAR ANTARCTICA, BUT NOT ON THE CONTI-
NENT. THEY BELONG TO A GROUP CALLED THE PYGOSCELID PENGUINS, WHICH ALSO
INCLUDES ADÉLIES AND GENTOOS. ALL THREE SPECIES FORM VERY LARGE
COLONIES—IN SOME CASES, PERHAPS A MILLION BIRDS.

accompanied British explorer James Cook on a voyage into the Antarctic Ocean in the 1770s, gave the gentoo its scientific name because he wrongly thought that it was the same as a bird found in New Guinea. Gentoo penguins live on subantarctic islands in the southern Atlantic, Indian, and Pacific Oceans. Like Adélies and chinstraps, gentoos eat krill, but they prey on larger fish as well. They stand about 30 inches (76 cm) tall and weigh

A PENGUIN COLONY IS NOT A QUIET PLACE. ONE GENTOO PENGUIN'S LOUD, HARSH CALL ISN'T TOO BAD—BUT MULTIPLY IT BY SEVERAL THOUSAND—OR SEVERAL HUNDRED THOUSAND—AND YOU CAN BEGIN TO SEE WHY MANY VISITORS HAVE BEEN STUNNED BY THE RACKET.

about 13 pounds (6 kg). Their characteristic marking is a white band or stripe that stretches over the top of the head from one eye to the other. Gentoos also have red-orange bills and feet.

Spheniscus Genus. The spheniscid penguins live farther north, in warmer waters whose temperatures rarely fall below about 45 degrees Fahrenheit (7.2 degrees Celsius). They are sometimes called the banded penguins because they have white bands or stripes on their heads and black bands across their upper chests. The four species are very similar in appearance and are identified by where they live rather than by distinctive markings. Spheniscids are also called burrowing penguins. All four spheniscid species nest underground, in holes or burrows that they find, steal from other penguins, or dig with their bills. Most people don't associate penguins with the desert, but the spheniscid penguins nest on the coastal fringes of some of the world's hottest and driest deserts.

The African penguin, *Spheniscus demersus*, was the first penguin known to Europeans: the one sighted by explorers sailing around southern Africa. It nests on the sandy shores and offshore islands of South Africa, as well as on the desert coast of the southwestern African nation of Namibia. African penguins are also called black-footed penguins for their black feet, or jackass penguins for their ear-piercing, braying, donkeylike cries. They average 24 inches (60 cm) in height and 8 pounds (3.5 kg) in weight and have a single black band across their upper chests. They cover distances of up to 75 miles (120 km) in search of food, mainly small fish but also shrimp and squid.

The Magellanic penguin, *Spheniscus magellanicus*, is the same height as the African but is slightly stockier and heavier. Magellanic penguins have double black bands on their upper chests. Their range includes the Falkland Islands and the coasts of Argentina, in southeastern South America, and Chile, in southwestern South America. They feed near the surface of the sea, where they prey on small fish.

The Humboldt penguin, *Spheniscus humboldti*, is also called the Peruvian penguin. Like the African, it has a single black band on its front. Humboldt penguins stand 22 inches (55 cm) tall and weigh an average of 10 pounds (4.5 kg). They nest in holes in the dry desert coastlands of Peru and Chile, from the Equator in the north to the city of Valparaiso in the south. Occasionally their territory overlaps that of the Magellanic penguins on South America's west coast. Huge numbers of Humboldt penguins once lived on the desert islands and rocks off the coast. There, the droppings of generations of seabirds formed thick layers of a white, powdery substance called guano, and Humboldts dug burrows in the guano. Beginning in the early nineteenth century, however, people dug up the guano for use as agricultural fertilizer, destroying much of the Humboldts' natural habitat and greatly reducing their numbers.

The fourth spheniscid species is the Galápagos penguin, *Spheniscus mendiculus*. It has two black chest bands, like the Magellanic penguin, and is the smallest spheniscid and second smallest of all penguins, standing about 18 inches (45 cm) tall and weighing 5 pounds (2.3 kg). It breeds in the Galápagos Islands, which are part of the South American nation of Ecuador. Primary nesting sites are on two of the larger islands, Fernandina and Isabela, but penguins occasionally appear on other islands in the group as well. Both the Galápagos and the Humboldt penguins feed near the ocean's surface. Their prey consists of anchovies and other small fish that live in vast schools in the Humboldt Current. Each winter a warm-water current called El Niño disturbs the Humboldt Current for a short time. Every seven years or so, the disturbance is greater, and the fish that normally support penguins and other seabirds disappear. At

HUMBOLDT PENGUINS HAVE LONG NESTED ON ROCKY OUTCROPPING AND ISLANDS LIKE THIS ONE ON THE COAST OF CHILE. THE WHITISH STAINS ON THE ROCK ARE GUANO, OR PENGUIN WASTE. PEOPLE HAVE STRIPPED THE GUANO OFF MANY ISLANDS FOR USE IN FERTILIZER, USUALLY DESTROYING THE BIRDS' NESTS IN THE PROCESS.

such times Humboldt and Galápagos penguins and their chicks may starve.

Eudyptes Genus. The genus *Eudyptes*, Latin for "good diver," contains six species of penguins. Three species live on sub-antarctic islands. Three live in milder waters near New Zealand. All six species are similar in appearance, with red eyes and tufts, or plumes, of yellow feathers that form crests above their eyes.

These distinctive plumes have earned the eudyptids the general name crested penguins. But although the eudyptid species are physically similar and in some cases occupy the same territories, they rarely mix, and never interbreed, in the wild.

The rockhopper penguin, *Eudyptes chrysocome*, has the largest range of the eudyptids. It nests on subantarctic islands in the Atlantic, Indian, and Pacific Oceans. Rockhoppers stand 18.5 inches (47 cm) tall and weigh 5.5 pounds (2.5 kg). They feed on krill and small fish caught near the surface of the ocean. Many rockhoppers nest on cliffs and plateaus above beaches. Stubby-legged and unable to fly, they climb to and from their nesting grounds in a series of short hops (so do some other penguin species that nest on high ground).

The macaroni penguin, *Eudyptes chrysolophus*, owes its common name to the eighteenth-century British slang term "macaroni," given to young gentlemen who favored fancy, Italian-influenced hairstyles and clothing. The floppy, long golden plumes of these penguins reminded explorers of the excessively stylish London youth. Macaroni penguins are found on many subantarctic islands and tend to live in very large colonies, sometimes numbering in the hundreds of thousands. They feed mainly on krill and stand about 24 inches (60 cm) tall, weighing 10 pounds (4.5 kg).

The royal penguin, *Eudyptes schlegeli*, is about the same size as the macaroni and also has a long golden crest. Royals eat more fish than macaronis—small fish make up about half their diet, krill and squid the rest. The royals' range is far smaller than that of the macaronis. Royal penguins are found only on Macquarie Island, south of Australia. A few scientists consider the macaroni and the royal to be the same species.

The remaining three species of eudyptids are sometimes called the New Zealand crested penguins. All three feed mainly

ROYAL PENGUINS ARE FOUND IN ONLY ONE PLACE ON EARTH: MACQUARIE ISLAND,
SOUTH OF AUSTRALIA. THEY ARE SO SIMILAR TO MACARONI PENGUINS THAT SOME
BIOLOGISTS CONSIDER ROYALS TO BE A SUBSPECIES OF MACARONI.

on krill, close to the surface and close to their breeding sites. They nest in holes or depressions among clumps of sea grass or under tree roots. The largest is the erect-crested penguin, *Eudyptes sclateri*, with an average height of 22.5 inches (57 cm) and a weight of 10 pounds (4.5 kg). Its home range includes the Bounty, Antipodes, and Auckland islands, three small island groups south of New Zealand, and Campbell Island, farther south. The Fiordland penguin, *Eudyptes pachyrhynchus*, is native to the Fiordland, a rain forest region on the southwest coast of New Zealand's South Island and on nearby Stewart Island. The Fiordland penguin's average height is 18.5 inches (47 cm); its average weight is 9 pounds (4 kg). The Snares penguin, *Eudyptes robustus*, is the same height as the Fiordland but weighs slightly more. It is found only on the wooded Snares Islands, south of New Zealand.

THE FIORDLAND PENGUIN IS ONE OF THREE SPECIES OF CRESTED PENGUINS FOUND IN NEW ZEALAND AND NEIGHBORING SMALL ISLANDS. NATIVE TO THE FORESTED FIORDLAND REGION OF SOUTHWESTERN NEW ZEALAND, IT IS VULNERABLE TO HUMAN ACTIVITY AND TO PREDATORS INTRODUCED BY PEOPLE. INTERNATIONAL CONSERVATION ORGANIZATIONS ESTIMATE THAT BETWEEN ONE THOUSAND AND FIVE THOUSAND PAIRS REMAIN.

***Megadyptes* Genus.** The genus *Megadyptes*—meaning "large diver"—contains a single species of penguin. It is the yellow-eyed penguin, *Megadyptes antipodes*, sometimes called the *hoiho*, the name given to it by the native Maori people of New Zealand. The name means "noise shouter" in Maori, and, like all penguins, these birds can be loud and raucous.

The yellow-eyed penguin differs from other penguins in several ways. Its back is blue-black and its front is white—typical for a penguin—but it has a pale brownish-yellow head and yellow eyes. Unlike all other penguins, it does not nest in colonies but in well-hidden, solitary burrows, often in dense forest. The yellow-eyed penguin measures 22 inches (56 cm) tall and weighs 12 pounds (5.5 kg). It can dive to depths of 165 feet (50 m) and lives on fish and squid. The rarest of all penguins, it lives along the southeastern coast of New Zealand and on Stewart Island, Campbell Island, and the Auckland Islands.

***Eudyptula* Genus.** The genus *Eudyptula*, or "good little diver," contains a single species, the world's smallest penguin. It is the little blue penguin, *Eudyptula minor*. The little blue is called the fairy penguin in Australia, where it lives on islands and beaches along the southern coast. It is Australia's only penguin. Little blues are also found on the coasts of New Zealand's North Island and South Island, as well as on the nearby Chatham Islands. Populations of little blue penguins in various parts of this range have minor differences in appearance, leading some scientists to classify them as distinct subspecies or even as several separate species.

Little blue penguins stand about 14 inches (35 cm) tall and weigh about 3 pounds (1.4 kg). They feed on small fish, small squid, and krill. They spend all day in the water, returning at night to their colonies, where they nest in burrows, under tree roots or porches, and in caves. In a few places in Australia, the

New Zealand's yellow-eyed penguin is named for one of its distinctive features. Its way of life also sets it apart from other penguins. Instead of forming colonies, yellow-eyed penguins live in isolated burrows. Their habitat is the rain forest—a far cry from the common image of penguins perched on icebergs.

The smallest penguin, the little blue, is the subject of penguin-protection campaigns in some communities in Australia and New Zealand. The birds have also become tourist attractions—crowds gather near nesting areas to watch the penguins going to or returning from the sea.

nightly parade of little blues hopping out of the sea and crossing the beach to reach their colonies has become a spectacle popular with tourists and locals alike.

Relatives

Scientists are not yet certain which families of living birds are penguins' closest relatives. Two families, the procellarids and the gaviids, appear to be good candidates. The procellarid family includes shearwaters and petrels, short-tailed pelagic birds found mostly in the Southern Hemisphere. The gaviid family includes loons, birds that swim and dive in both salt and fresh water and nest close to the water.

Another family of birds, the alcids, is more distantly related to penguins, yet resembles them more closely than either the procellarids or the gaviids. The alcid family includes puffins, auks, and murres, chunky-bodied, short-winged, upright-standing black-and-white seabirds that swim by using their wings underwater, as penguins do. Alcids live in much the same way in the northern part of the Northern Hemisphere as penguins do in the southern part of the Southern Hemisphere. Puffins, in fact, are sometimes called the penguins of the North. Unlike penguins, however, alcids can fly.

The many similarities in appearance and behavior between alcids and penguins are examples of what biologists call convergent evolution. Two distinct groups of organisms, living in widely separated parts of the world, have evolved to look and act very much alike because they occupy almost identical ecological niches. They nest in similar places, swim in similar waters, and eat similar food. Penguins, however, have sacrificed the ability to fly in order to become somewhat more efficient than alcids at diving and swimming. Why haven't alcids also lost the power of

PUFFINS—SOMETIMES CALLED THE PENGUINS OF THE NORTH—OCCUPY HABITATS AND ECOLOGICAL NICHES SIMILAR TO THOSE OF SOME PENGUIN SPECIES. PUFFINS ARE FOUND ONLY IN THE NORTHERN HEMISPHERE, PENGUINS IN THE SOUTHERN.

flight? The answer may lie in zoogeography, which is the science of how different kinds of animals are distributed across the world. The northern reaches of the Northern Hemisphere, where alcids live, are home to many land predators: polar bears, wolves, foxes—even people. Flight is the best way to escape such predators. But the Southern Hemisphere has no large land predators. Birds, fish, and marine mammals prey on penguins, but penguins face fewer threats on land than alcids do. This may be why alcids still fly and penguins can only waddle, hop, and swim.

3

The Physical Penguin

"His element is the sea," wrote Cherry Kearton in *The Island of Penguins* (1930), a study of Magellanic penguins on Dassen Island, South Africa. "When you see him floating, he is no longer comical but entirely beautiful, resting on the moving water, with head raised, a little like a duck; then he suddenly decides to swim, down goes his head, out go his flippers, and like a flash he slips through the water, a streak of black just below the surface."

Penguins evolved to live in the water, not in the air or on land. Still, they share many features of basic bird biology. Some of their physical features, however, are special adaptations—departures from ordinary bird biology that have evolved to fit penguins to their way of life. These adaptations make penguins excellent swimmers and help them adjust to extreme temperatures.

MANY OBSERVERS HAVE NOTED THAT A LAND-BOUND PENGUIN'S COMICAL CLUMSINESS VANISHES AS SOON AS THE BIRD ENTERS THE WATER, ITS NATURAL ELEMENT. SWIFT AND SLEEK, PENGUINS FLY AND SOAR UNDERWATER AS OTHER BIRDS DO IN THE SKY.

Basic Bird Biology

The simplest definition of a bird is that it is an animal with feathers. All birds have feathers, although some have more than others, and no other animals have them. Most birds have two kinds of feathers: vanes (stiff feathers with central stems) and down (soft, fluffy, warm feathers without central stems). A penguin's feathers are a combination of the two types. The base of each feather consists of two quills or shafts. One sprouts down. The other supports a small, stiff vane. These feathers are packed closely together—as many as eighty per square inch in the densely feathered emperor penguins—and the vanes overlap like the scales of a fish. A third type of feather, the plume, is long and flexible. Often brightly colored, it creates distinctive markings and is sometimes used to attract mates. Among penguins, only the crested penguins have plumes: their yellow "eyebrow" tufts.

Feathers are fragile. They break and become worn. At least once each year, birds grow new feathers, which push the old ones out as they emerge. In some species, this regrowing and shedding occurs all year, a few feathers at a time. Other species regrow all of their feathers at the same time—a process called molting. Penguins molt. Once each year a penguin begins to look swollen and scruffy as its old feathers get pushed out of the way by the new, emerging ones. The whole process takes from two to four weeks. Penguins cannot enter the water until their new coats of feathers are complete, so throughout the molt they don't swim and they don't eat. They simply stand around, shedding feathers like ruptured pillows, until the process is completed, after which they scurry to the sea to make up for lost time.

All birds preen, or groom their feathers with their bills, straightening and cleaning them. Some birds, including penguins, have organs called uropygial glands that produce oil used

A MOLTING ROCKHOPPER PENGUIN. FOUND ON MANY ROCKY ISLANDS IN THE SOUTHERN OCEANS, ROCKHOPPERS OWE THEIR NAME TO THE LONG JOURNEYS MANY OF THEM MAKE OVER STEEP TERRAIN TO REACH THEIR NESTS. SHORT OF LEG, UNABLE TO FLY, THEY PROGRESS IN A SERIES OF ABRUPT HOPS.

THESE FALKLAND ISLANDS KING PENGUINS ARE MOLTING, SHEDDING OLD FEATHERS TO REVEAL NEW ONES. THEY WON'T BE ABLE TO SWIM—OR CATCH FOOD—UNTIL THE MOLT IS COMPLETE, WHICH CAN TAKE UP TO A MONTH.

in preening. The uropygial gland is located on a bird's back, just above the tail. The bird rubs the gland with its bill and then uses its bill to spread oil on its feathers while preening. Penguins have unusually large uropygial glands that provide enough oil to completely waterproof their entire bodies. They usually preen before and after each swim or dive.

EMPEROR PENGUINS HAVE AS MANY AS EIGHTY FEATHERS PER SQUARE INCH, MORE
THAN ANY OTHER PENGUIN SPECIES. OVERLAPPING LIKE THE SCALES OF A FISH, THE
FEATHERS ARE ADAPTED TO KEEP THE BIRDS BOTH WARM AND DRY.

Penguins' internal systems are much like those of other birds. The nervous system consists of the brain and the nerves, which carry information to and from the brain. The circulatory system consists of the heart, which pumps blood, and the blood vessels, which carry blood throughout the body. The respiratory system brings oxygen into the body. Like mammals, birds breathe through their mouths and noses. And as in mammals, oxygen from the air enters the bloodstream through organs

Penguin Internal Organs

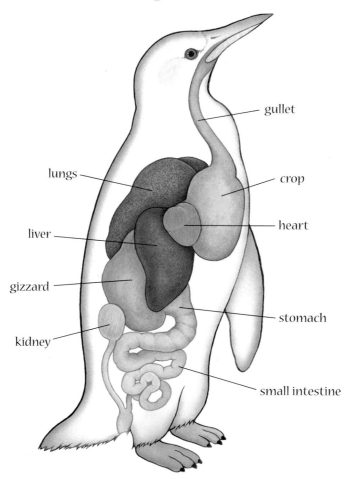

gullet

lungs

crop

heart

liver

gizzard

stomach

kidney

small intestine

called lungs. However, birds' respiratory systems include organs not found in mammals. These are small pouches, or sacs, nested among the birds' other internal organs. When a bird inhales, some air enters these sacs instead of the lungs. The air in the sacs cools the organs to keep them from overheating—a necessary feature because birds have no sweat glands and can't lower their body temperatures by perspiring.

Penguins absorb nourishment and eliminate waste through their digestive systems. They capture live food, but they don't have teeth to bite it or chew it. Instead, their tongues and the insides of their mouths are covered with fleshy but strong barbs, or short spines, that point down the throat. Once prey enters the mouth, it cannot escape past these barbs. Penguins that feed on large prey, such as squid and good-sized fish, also have sharp-edged hooked bills to help in the capture.

Food passes through the penguin's esophagus, or throat, into an organ called the crop. Many birds have crops, which they use for storing food if the stomach is full or for carrying food back to the young. All penguins use their crops to store food. The emperor can carry the largest load—up to 9 pounds (4 kg). The smallest penguins, the little blues, can store 2.6 ounces (75 g) of food in their crops.

If a penguin does not regurgitate from its crop to feed its chick, the food will move into the bird's two-part stomach. In the first part, digestive juices soften the food. Then, in the second, muscles in the stomach walls grind it. The next stage in the digestive system is the small intestine, which absorbs nutrients from the food. What remains goes on to the large intestine, where the water it contains is absorbed into the penguin's body. The penguin excretes the remaining waste through an opening called the vent, located in the rear of its body. Penguins also rid themselves of waste matter another way. Like other seagoing

LIKE THE BARBS INSIDE ITS MOUTH, THE PENGUIN'S HOOKED BEAK HELPS IT KEEP HOLD OF ITS PREY. THIS AFRICAN PENGUIN FEEDS ON SMALL FISH, SQUID, AND SHRIMP.

A GENTOO PENGUIN FEEDING ITS CHICK. PENGUIN CHICKS GROW EXTREMELY RAPIDLY AND REQUIRE LARGE AMOUNTS OF FOOD, USUALLY PROVIDED BY BOTH PARENTS.

birds, they drink salt water. Their heads contain small organs called salt glands that remove the salt from the water so that the bird's body can absorb freshwater. The salt leaves the penguin's body in the form of a thick liquid that drips out of the nostrils.

Birds have no external sex organs. All parts of their reproductive systems are located inside their bodies. In males, sex organs called testes produce sperm. The testes are connected to the vent, through which the sperm will leave the bird's body. In female birds, sex organs called ovaries produce eggs. Most species of birds breed at particular seasons. As the breeding season approaches, the testes and ovaries become larger. Within the female, eggs leave the ovaries and enter an organ called the oviduct, which is connected to the vent. When it is time to mate, the male gets on top of and behind the female, and the two position their vents next to each other. Sperm leaves the male's vent and enters the female's, where it fertilizes one or more of the eggs in the oviduct. Once an egg is fertilized, a shell forms around it. The female lays the egg by passing it out of the oviduct through the vent.

Super Swimmers

Many of penguins' characteristic features allow them not just to survive but to thrive in a marine environment. Adaptations of their skeletons have made them outstanding swimmers, while the coloring of their plumage is ideal for the watery world where they spend much of their time.

Birds' skeletons differ from those of other animals in several important ways. For one thing, birds' bones are hollow. This lessens the amount of weight that flying birds have to carry aloft. For another, birds' sternums, or breastbones, have bony, blade-shaped projections called keels. Birds require large, powerful muscles to move their wings, and those muscles are anchored to the keels. In flightless land birds, such as ostriches, the keels have almost disappeared. But although penguins do not fly, they still have large, strong keels. That's because they use their wings underwater, where they must press against more resistance than they would encounter if they were flying through air. Penguins' wing muscles are extremely powerful. "A full-grown emperor penguin," reports William Ashworth in *Penguins, Puffins, and Auks*, "is quite capable of breaking human leg bones with a blow of its wing." Penguins also have solid, heavy bones, unlike other

Penguin Skeleton

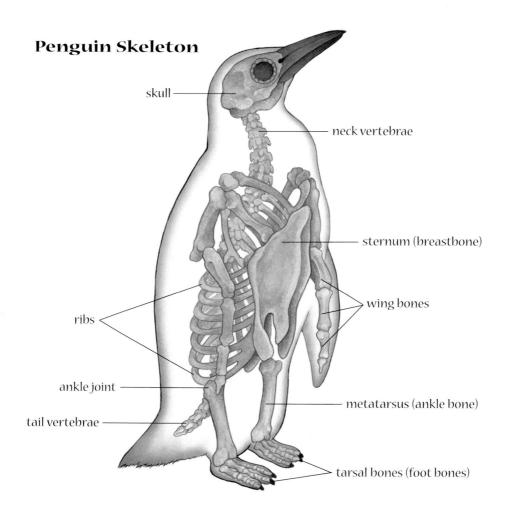

skull

neck vertebrae

sternum (breastbone)

wing bones

ribs

ankle joint

metatarsus (ankle bone)

tail vertebrae

tarsal bones (foot bones)

birds. Penguins don't need to be light enough to be supported in the air—they need to be heavy enough not to keep bobbing to the surface of the water.

Like other animals, birds have four limbs. A bird's limbs consist of two legs and two limbs that have become modified into wings. Most birds have four toes on each foot, and birds that swim often have webs of skin between the toes to make the feet more efficient as paddles. Penguins, however, have three toes on each foot, each tipped with a claw. Penguins' toes are webbed, but penguins do not use their feet as paddles when they swim, as some water birds do. Instead, they propel themselves through the water with their wings, using their feet and tails as rudders for steering and changing direction. Some scientists think that penguins' short, thick legs and three-toed feet evolved to reduce the surface area of legs and feet—the amount of bare skin exposed to cold water while the birds are swimming. In addition, the short legs keep the feet close to the body, not trailing behind it. This means that slight changes in the angle of the feet instantly alter the direction the penguin is swimming, making penguins nimble and maneuverable swimmers. The strong muscles needed to move the legs against the resistance of water are attached to bony projections called enemial crests on penguins' knees.

Penguins' wings have evolved into flippers, much like those of some marine mammals. They are short, narrow, and streamlined. The wing bones have become flattened and fused, or fastened together, so that the wings remain stiff, like paddles. Unlike other birds, penguins cannot fold their wings over their backs. They must hold them at their sides, which makes the wings look a bit like arms and increases the upright-walking penguins' resemblance to people.

The penguin's overall shape makes it an excellent swimmer.

Penguin Body

When designing torpedoes and other things intended to travel underwater, engineers often use a shape very similar to that of the emperor penguin—a streamlined profile with a narrow front end and the greatest thickness about one-third of the way along the length. This shape—called a fusiform, or spindle-shaped profile—moves through water with the least possible resistance.

Penguins' black-backed, white-fronted coloring is very noticeable on land. But in the water, where penguins face the greatest danger from predators, it provides a type of camouflage known as countershading. Seen from above, the penguin's dark back is lost in the dark, murky waters where the bird makes its home. Seen from below, its light front appears to blend into the pale surface where the sea meets the sky.

Coping with Cold and Heat

A penguin's normal body temperature is around 100 degrees Fahrenheit (38 degrees Celsius). Penguins maintain that temperature—staying warm in cold conditions and cool in hot conditions—with physical adaptations and behavior.

Feathers play a vital role in temperature control. They trap air next to the skin, where it becomes warm. The downy part of each feather provides more warmth and insulation, while the scalelike vaned tips of the feathers form a tight covering that keeps water and wind away from the down and skin beneath. Another insulating feature is the layer of fat beneath the penguin's skin. In Antarctic species, such as the emperors and Adélies, as much as one-third of a penguin's body weight may consist of fat. The Antarctic penguins also have the densest and longest feathers of the penguin family. These penguins have developed habits that help them stay warm. They bask in the sun when it is available, and they crowd together in large groups to share and conserve body heat.

In spite of the common image of penguins as birds of ice and snow, penguins can overheat. When the most northerly species come ashore, they land on the hot shores of the tropical Galápagos Islands or the desert coasts of western South America and Africa. Heat can also be a problem in southern Australia and New Zealand. On the subantarctic islands and even in Antarctica, hot, sunny days call for careful temperature management if penguins are to avoid overheating. If a penguin

becomes overheated, it risks heatstroke. For some penguins, such as Adélies, this can happen when the temperature rises above freezing.

All penguins have built-in cooling mechanisms. When they raise or ruffle their feathers slightly, the warm air trapped beneath the feathers escapes, cooling the bird. At the same time, the tiny blood vessels beneath the skin widen, allowing more blood to flow through them and release its heat into the atmosphere. Penguins can also release heat from their bodies by lying on their stomachs with the bare soles of their feet exposed to the air or by raising their wings to let heat leave their bodies from a network of blood vessels on the wings' undersides. In some species, the "underarms" flush pink when the penguins cool themselves this way. In addition, penguins that live in mild or warm climates have less dense plumage than the southern species, and most of them have bare patches around the bill or the eyes to help them release heat. These more northerly penguin species also stay cool by swimming during the day to avoid

ADÉLIE PENGUINS CROSS A GLACIER IN THE SOUTH ORKNEY ISLANDS, NORTH OF THE ANTARCTIC PENINSULA. ADÉLIES ALSO LIVE ON THE ANTARCTIC CONTINENT ITSELF. THEY ARE THE ONLY PENGUINS OTHER THAN EMPERORS TO DO SO.

the burning sun and by burrowing, making their nests under shady cover rather than in the open sun. Managing body temperature is part of adapting to life in extreme conditions— something penguins have done very well.

4 A Penguin's Life

Ornithologist Roger Tory Peterson noted that "many of the things that go on in a crowded penguin city seem strikingly human. There is constant bickering with neighbors; fights erupt for no apparent reason; and the cacophony of greeting, protest, and challenge is deafening. And yet it is not all chaos; there is a definite pattern of behavior, a social system. . . ."

Captive penguins often live for thirty years or so. In the wild, a penguin's maximum life span is about twenty years. During that time the penguin copes with the challenges and events that shape the lives of all creatures. Penguins interact with others of their own kind, they mate and raise young, they eat and try not to get eaten. These activities take place in a colony that may number as few as several dozen birds or as many as a million. From birth to death, most penguins live their lives within communities.

CHINSTRAP PENGUINS LOOK DAPPER AND DIGNIFIED, BUT THEIR EXCEPTIONALLY LOUD CRIES HAVE EARNED THEM THE NICKNAME "STONECRACKER" PENGUINS.

Communities

Scientists don't yet know a great deal about how groups of penguins behave when they are at sea feeding—for months on end, in some species. Experts who have studied penguins do know that the birds generally swim, travel, and feed together. Even when they spread out and appear to be acting as individuals, they are usually close to others of their own kind. But further study of penguins at sea is needed to answer questions about how they interact in the water. Much more is known about penguins' group behavior on land, where they have been observed for decades.

Penguins' main activities on land are mating, nesting, and raising their young. They do so in areas called breeding grounds, where they gather in groups called colonies. Some of these communities have existed since the first scientific observers noticed them a century or more ago. Penguin colonies tend to use the same breeding grounds each year. Wildlife observers have found that some individual penguins or mated pairs even return to the same nest spot within the breeding ground. Some penguins, especially those that live in northerly or mild climates, never wander far from their breeding grounds and may come ashore daily. The yellow-eyed and Galápagos penguins, for example, occupy their colonies more or less year-round. Other species, such as the Adélies and emperors, visit their breeding grounds only during the mating and breeding season.

The size and organization of penguin colonies vary widely. At one extreme are the shy yellow-eyed penguins of southern New Zealand. These penguins form small, scattered colonies of a few dozen, or at most a few hundred, pairs. Each pair nests far from all the others. In Australia, little blue penguins follow a similar pattern: a few hundred burrows or hidden nests widely scattered across a breeding ground. The burrowing penguins of

EMPEROR PENGUINS BILLING. TOUCHING BILLS OR RUBBING THEM TOGETHER IS PART OF COURTSHIP BEHAVIOR, THE PREPARATION FOR MATING AND REARING A FAMILY.

Peru and the Galápagos Islands also gather in colonies ranging in size from a few dozen to several hundred pairs. Among the crested penguins, macaronis and royals form very large colonies, sometimes numbering in the hundreds of thousands of birds. Kings and emperors also form large colonies. These two species, the largest, do not build nests. Instead, the parents carry their eggs on their feet. King and emperor colonies are sometimes so crowded that each bird is surrounded by only as much space as it can clear with its sharp bill.

The three pygoscelid species—Adélie, chinstrap, and gentoo—are all very social penguins, living in close-packed colonies that number from a few dozen to hundreds of thousands of birds. Observers have estimated that some colonies hold more than a million penguins. Penguins may be adorable birds, as many people think, but the first sight (and smell) of a large penguin colony is something of a shock. Just as with large human populations, such immense gatherings of penguins produce sewage and noise. Edward Wilson, a member of British explorer Robert Falcon Scott's 1902 Antarctic expedition, described an immense colony of Adélies he saw at Cape Adare on the Ross Sea coast of Antarctica:

> *Such a sight! There were literally millions of them. They covered the plain which was nearly 200 acres in extent, and they covered the slopes of Cape Adare above the plain, to the very top. . . . The place was the color of anchovy paste from the excreta of the young penguins. It simply stunk like hell, and the noise was deafening.*

Wilson's description is echoed by some of the more recent visitors to the large Antarctic and subantarctic penguin colonies. Writes James Gorman in *The Total Penguin*, "Noise is one of the two overwhelming realities of life in a penguin colony." The second overwhelming reality is the odor of penguin excrement, or guano. When thousands of penguins relieve themselves day after day in the same small area, the result is unavoidable: penguins spend much of their time on land standing in their own waste. If the penguins' diet consists of large amounts of krill, shrimps, and other shellfish, as is often the case, the guano will have a pinkish tinge, and so will some of the penguins—at least until their next swim. Gorman reports that some large penguin colonies can be spotted from space "by the pink or white guano patches on dark rock."

Like other creatures that live in communities, penguins have ways of communicating with each other. They express themselves with both voice and body language. Ornithologists refer to penguins as highly vocal, which means that they use their voices a lot. Studies have shown that the larger the size of a penguin colony, the more often and the more loudly individual penguins vocalize. In other words, as things get more crowded, they make more noise.

Penguins vocalize to identify themselves to family members. Even in the midst of thousands of vocalizing penguins, adult penguins appear to recognize the voices of their mates and their chicks. Adélie penguins regularly pick their young out of large crowds of identical chicks, and most experts think that they do so by voice recognition. But penguins also "speak" to those outside their families. Depending upon the species, they squawk, trumpet, or make sounds that resemble the barking of dogs or the braying of donkeys. And depending upon the circumstances, these sounds can be meant to attract a mate or to signal aggression toward a rival, a neighbor who has wandered too close, or a would-be predator. Often penguins vocalize for no clear reason—at least, none that wildlife scientists can identify.

Most penguin species, especially those that form very large colonies, have developed ways of getting along with the neighbors. One of the most important of these is what observers call the "slender walk." When a penguin has to worm its way among many close-packed neighbors or nesting pairs to reach its own little territory within the colony, it walks with its head and tail lowered, its shoulders pulled forward, its wings held stiffly in front of it, and its feathers flattened, as if trying to make itself as small and inoffensive as possible. It looks as though the penguin is trying to say, "Please excuse me, I don't want to start any trouble. I'm just trying to get through." A completely different message comes from the "advertising walk" that males of some species, especially king penguins, perform when they want to attract the attention of possible mates. They ruffle their feathers and swagger proudly around, swiveling their necks as if to show off their colorful head markings. Observers have given the name ecstatic display or ecstatic vocalization to another common penguin behavior, one performed both by individuals and by mated pairs. A penguin performing an ecstatic display points its bill toward the sky (except for the little blue, which points it forward, and the emperor, which points it down), stretches its neck, holds

BIOLOGISTS HAVE SPENT COUNTLESS HOURS STUDYING COLONIES SUCH AS THIS VAST COMMUNITY OF KING PENGUINS, AND THEY HAVE LEARNED MUCH ABOUT THE BIRDS' INTERACTIONS AND SOCIAL BEHAVIOR—ON LAND. LITTLE IS YET KNOWN, HOWEVER, ABOUT HOW PENGUINS INTERACT AND BEHAVE AT SEA, WHERE THEY SPEND MOST OF THEIR TIME.

its wings out to its sides, and shakes while giving out loud cries. These displays seem to be used for several purposes. Sometimes they announce ownership of a nest or territory, while at other times they are a bonding ritual between mates.

Sometimes communication breaks down and fights break out, usually when conditions are crowded or when one penguin has stolen a nest site or a piece of nesting material from another. Penguins strike each other with their wings and peck savagely at each other with their bills, but fights are rarely fatal. Often, in fact, the fight ends before it begins, when one penguin backs down in the face of a wing-flapping, lunging display of aggression from the other.

In some parts of the penguin's range, several species live close together, sometimes in neighboring or overlapping territories. Adélie, gentoo, and chinstrap penguins, for example, live together on Antarctica's Palmer Peninsula. Sometimes the three even share colonies. Yet they hunt in slightly different parts of the offshore waters, and they never attempt to interbreed. Each type of penguin tends to stick with those of its own type. Some biologists believe that penguins can tell their own species from other similar ones by the distinctive markings and coloration that have evolved on each species. These markings, located on the head, neck, and upper chest, are readily visible when penguins are swimming at the surface of the water with their heads in the air, as well as on land and underwater.

Family Life

Family life begins with courtship between a male and a female penguin. The male's goal is to attract a mate so that he can breed. In some species, he doesn't have much time—the farther south a penguin lives, the shorter the breeding season. Chicks must be born early in the southern summer so that they will be strong enough to survive the coming winter.

Males try to attract females by vocalizing; by using special postures, such as the ecstatic display, or special walks, such as the advertising walk, and sometimes by tending nests. Adélies, for example, build nests out of pebbles, and males go to great lengths to get and guard the pebbles, often stealing them from neighbors. Among species that do not build nests, such as kings and emperors, a male may stake out a patch of territory and defend it, hoping that it will attract a mate.

Male and female penguins show their interest in one another through courtship behavior, which varies from species to species. Adélies stare at each other sidelong as they bow. Kings click their bills as *they* bow. Emperors walk side by side. Rockhoppers and other crested species shake their heads. Penguins also walk around each other in circles that grow smaller and smaller until the birds are touching each other's sides, vocalize together, and rub their bills together. Billing looks much like kissing, and it is most common among newly joined pairs. The pair may also groom each other. Courtship displays may continue for several hours, or even longer, before the birds mate. After they mate, courtship behavior may continue, at least in some form. Whenever a pair has been separated—if one partner has been at sea feeding, for example, while the other has been minding the nest—they greet one another with cries, bows, and perhaps billing.

Some of the first scientific studies of penguins reported that the birds mated for life. This "fact" about penguins is widely repeated, but it isn't true. Some penguins do mate for life—or at least year after year until one partner dies. But studies have shown that penguins often mate with new partners even when the old ones are still alive and in the same colony. In one

AN AFRICAN PENGUIN RETURNS TO ITS NEST WITH BUILDING MATERIAL. SOME PENGUIN SPECIES BUILD NO NESTS AT ALL, SOME DIG HOLES OR BURROWS, AND SOME BUILD SIMPLE NESTS BY ASSEMBLING STICKS OR STONES ON THE GROUND.

emperor colony at Cape Crozier, Antarctica, for example, only 14 percent of males mated with the same female two years in a row. Between 50 and 80 percent of Adélie penguins remain paired with the same mates from one year to the next. In addition, observers have learned that some male and female penguins occasionally "cheat" on their partners, even while they are nesting and raising young together, by mating with other penguins.

Most penguin species mate in the southern spring, in September and October, and raise their young during the southern summer, from November through February. Little blues breed a month or two earlier, and Humboldts and Galápagos penguins may breed at any time of the year. And the two large penguins of the *Aptenodytes* genus, the kings and emperors, face a special breeding challenge. Because they are so large, their eggs take longer to gestate in the female's body and longer to incubate on the nest than those of other penguins. And their chicks take longer to reach maturity than other penguin chicks. Kings and emperors have solved this problem in different ways, although each produces only one chick at a time.

British scientist Bernard Stonehouse figured out the complex breeding cycle of king penguins. While other penguin species rear their young in a twelve-month cycle, kings have a breeding cycle of fifteen months, which they repeat twice in each three-year period. The first year they breed very early in the breeding season, which means that they finish raising that year's chick near the end of the second year's breeding season. As a result, they breed late in the season of the second year. During the breeding season of the third year they are still raising the second year's chick, so they don't breed at all. They begin again early in the breeding season of the fourth year. This means that kings produce two chicks every three years.

Emperor penguins have managed to keep their breeding

cycle down to twelve months, but at a high cost. In order to rear their young in spring and summer, they mate in March, the Antarctic autumn. Females lay their eggs in May and then leave for the open sea. For two months the male emperors huddle together for warmth on the sea ice, each holding its egg on its feet. Warmth for the egg is provided by the brood pouch, a fold of feathered skin on the lower abdomen that the male drapes over the egg. During this time the male emperors neither swim nor eat—they simply survive. The chicks hatch in July, the depth of the Antarctic winter. Kept warm by their fathers' feet and brood pouches, the infant emperors survive on a liquid that the males regurgitate from their crops. Finally, two or three months after leaving, the females return to take over the care of the chicks, and the males—who have lost at least one-third of their body weight—can go to the ocean to feed.

Emperor penguins are the only creatures known to breed and to incubate eggs in the months-long darkness, bitter cold, and lashing winds of the Antarctic winter. The conditions that male emperors endure are summed up in the title of a book written by Apsley Cherry-Garrard about a three-week journey that he and two other men made in the winter of 1911 to collect emperor penguin eggs. He called the adventure *The Worst Journey in the World*.

Female king and emperor penguins lay one egg each breeding season. All other species produce two eggs. Among the crested penguins, though, one egg is smaller than the other, and the parents may incubate only the larger egg. In cases where both chicks hatch, the larger and stronger one usually survives. The parents generally do not feed the smaller chick, which dies. Some biologists think that the secondary, smaller offspring is a form of insurance for crested penguins. If a predator seizes the primary egg or chick, the nesting pair can turn their attention to

King penguins are brooding their eggs, which are tucked away between the birds' feet and their brood pouches. One egg has rolled away from its parents. If they do not recover it quickly, cold or a predatory bird will end their chances of producing young this year.

the secondary one and still produce a chick for the season.

Aside from emperors, kings, and crested penguins, the other species try to raise two chicks each season. Males and females share equally in the duties of parenthood. They take turns incubating the egg and feeding the always-hungry chick, all the while trying to protect their offspring from predators such as gulls. Among some species, such as kings, emperors, and Adélies, slightly older chicks cluster together in large groups called nurseries, or crèches, allowing both parents to feed at the same time. Males and females alike feed their young regurgitated food from their crops. The food is partly digested and packed into small balls. To get it, chicks put their open bills inside those of their parents.

Chicks are covered with extremely fluffy gray-and-white down feathers. At the end of the breeding season, they molt and acquire their first coat of true plumage, with waterproof feathers. Its coloration is like that of the adults, but lighter. At this time, the young penguins are considered juveniles. They are separated from their parents, who may already have gone to sea weeks earlier, and they are now ready to take the plunge into their own seagoing lives. A year later, at their second molt, juveniles get full adult plumage. Sometimes, however, they do not achieve full adult status for another year or so. It may take a young penguin several breeding seasons to attract mates and begin raising young. Until that time, some young penguins

A KING PENGUIN PARENT PREPARES TO TRANSFER THE EGG TO ITS MATE'S FEET. MALE AND FEMALE PENGUINS SHARE CHILD-CARE DUTIES AND CONTRIBUTE EQUALLY TO FEEDING THE YOUNG.

An emperor penguin pair and their chick. Because of the heavy demands of rearing young in the harsh Antarctic climate, emperors breed only two years out of every three.

WITH THEIR THICK DOWNY PLUMAGE AND THEIR RAPID WEIGHT GAIN, YOUNG PENGUINS SOMETIMES APPEAR LARGER THAN THEIR ATTENTIVE PARENTS.

wander about on their own within the colony, or even from colony to colony. Others form little gangs or bands that pick fights and disturb nests. Some observers have called these restless young troublemakers hooligans. The hooligans settle down into respectable adulthood when they acquire mates.

Prey and Predators

Much of every penguin's life consists of a search for food. Penguins eat only at sea (except for food caught at sea and carried to land in their crops), and some of them range very far in search of prey. Emperor penguins have been known to swim for up to 600 miles (1,000 kilometers) on a single hunting trip and to dive to depths of 1,300 feet (400 m). Most penguins, though, stay closer to home. Even kings, the second-largest penguins, usually travel only about 20 miles (30 km) from their colonies in the quest for food. Macaroni and royal penguins also stay within about 20 miles (30 km) of their colonies, while African penguins travel more than three times as far. A few species feed in offshore waters so close to their breeding grounds that they come ashore daily.

A penguin at sea, snapping up its prey, is likely to become a meal for a larger predator. The chief danger comes from marine mammals: seals, sea lions, and orcas (also called killer whales, orcas rarely eat any penguin smaller than an emperor). Without a doubt the Antarctic leopard seal, *Hydrurga leptonyx*, is the deadliest predator of the penguin species that inhabit the Antarctic Ocean. Penguins appear to be one of the leopard seal's favorite foods. According to William Ashworth, author of *Penguins, Puffins, and Auks*, "Leopard seals have a rather chilling way of grasping a bird by its feet and, with a violent head snap, jerking it completely out of its skin—certainly not among the prettier ways to die." These sleek, fast-moving seals often lurk in the waters near penguin colonies or icebergs with penguins on them, waiting for a chance to snatch birds when they are easiest to catch and most vulnerable—as they enter or leave the water. Scientists think that one reason penguins generally enter and leave the ocean in large groups is the principle of "safety in

THIS KING PENGUIN'S CHICK WILL SOON RECEIVE ITS FIRST ADULT PLUMAGE AND
BEGIN LIFE ON ITS OWN.

ONCE THEY ARE OLD ENOUGH TO LEAVE THEIR FATHER'S BROOD POUCHES, EMPEROR PENGUIN CHICKS MAY HUDDLE TOGETHER IN GROUPS CALLED NURSERIES. THE CONTACT HELPS THE YOUNG BIRDS STAY WARM WHILE THEIR PARENTS ARE BUSY FEEDING.

numbers." An individual's chances of escaping a predator are greater if the individual is lost in a crowd.

Sharks and other big fish also prey on penguins. So do dolphins and porpoises from time to time. Large crabs devour Galápagos chicks. But the greatest threat to penguins doesn't come from the land or even the sea. It comes from the air, the element that penguins abandoned long ago in their evolution. Predatory birds eat enormous numbers of penguin eggs and chicks. Among the largest and fiercest of the winged predators are the skuas, large brown birds that are related to gulls but

A SHEATHBILL TRIES TO STEAL THE FOOD THAT A KING PENGUIN IS REGURGITATING FOR ITS YOUNG. SMALL PREDATORY BIRDS ATTACK THE PENGUINS' FOOD AT SUCH TIMES. LARGER ONES ATTACK PENGUIN CHICKS WHO ARE LOST OR UNGUARDED.

also have some characteristics of hawks. Skuas occasionally work in pairs or even larger teams, distracting parent birds so that one of them can slip into the nest and make off with the egg or chick. Any chick that wanders away from its nest is at risk of being picked off by one of these birds, which lurk around all Antarctic penguin colonies. Other birds also prey on penguin eggs and chicks, and sometimes on sick or wounded adult penguins. These include various species of gulls, sheathbills (white birds that resemble pigeons), and giant fulmars, seabirds whose wingspan may be 7 feet (2 m). Penguins in the Falkland

Islands may fall victim to caracaras, South American birds that are similar to falcons.

Movement on Land and at Sea

Don't let the waddling gait of the penguin fool you. Although penguins look clumsy on land, and they are in some ways out of their element there, they can move surprisingly fast. They cannot run fast for long distances, but they can outrun people over short distances. And they are sturdy walkers, in spite of their short legs. Often they walk, climb, or hop for several miles over rough, uneven ground to reach their nest sites.

Sometimes, though, there is an easier way to travel. When a penguin has to move across snow, it may drop onto its stomach and glide forward, propelling itself with its wings and feet in a movement called tobogganing (a toboggan is a type of sled). Penguins can move faster by tobogganing than by walking.

Penguins at sea move so smoothly and effortlessly that they often seem to be swimming faster than is really the case. When early explorers and hunters, and even some scientists, estimated how fast penguins were swimming, they almost always came up with figures that modern researchers consider too high. Careful studies of birds wearing radio transmitters have shown that most penguins swim at 4 to 5 miles (6.4 to 8 km) an hour when they are feeding, about the same speed as a fast human walker or a jogger travels. Penguins traveling over long distances may go even more slowly, while those with a need for speed—perhaps to escape predators—can swim faster for short periods.

At sea, penguins usually travel in groups, perhaps for safety in numbers. Unless they are diving in search of food, they tend to swim near the surface of the water. Penguins need to breathe every minute or so. They can breathe in one of two ways: by

PENGUINS USUALLY ENTER AND LEAVE THE SEA IN LARGE GROUPS, AND SOME
BIOLOGISTS THINK THIS IS FOR "SAFETY IN NUMBERS." BY BLENDING INTO A CROWD,
AN INDIVIDUAL PENGUIN MAY AVOID CATCHING THE ATTENTION OF A PREDATOR SUCH
AS A WAITING LEOPARD SEAL.

sticking their heads out of the water or by leaping out of the water while continuing to travel forward, as porpoises and dolphins do. Known as porpoising, this move has an advantage. Air offers less resistance to forward motion than water does, so penguins save a little energy by porpoising as they travel along. It is as close as they can come to flying through the air.

Some penguins feed on prey found near the surface, but others dive more deeply. Most penguin dives last a minute or two. Their maximum depth is 230 to 330 feet (70 to 100 m), although the majority of dives are much shallower. Emperors and kings, however, can dive much deeper and for longer periods. Emperors have been known to reach depths of more than 1,000 feet (350 m), farther below the sea's surface than any other bird. One measured dive by an emperor penguin lasted eighteen minutes, although four minutes is more typical. Like many other aspects of penguins' lives at sea, the physical adaptations that allow emperor penguins to make such deep, long dives are not yet understood by researchers.

5 People and Penguins

T he greatest threat to penguins' long-term survival is neither leopard seals nor skuas. It is people. As hunters, polluters, and competitors for food and territory, human beings have killed penguins or made their lives more difficult. Yet people have also labored to save penguins from oil spills and other disasters, to preserve their habitats, and to protect them. Today, the future of penguins, like the future of most life on earth, depends in large part on the willingness of people to share the planet and its resources with other species.

Serious Slaughter

People and penguins lived together for many years in places like New Zealand and coastal Africa and South America. People hunted penguins and their eggs for food, although wildlife historians don't know much about how this early hunting affected penguin populations. As long as human populations remained

A TANKER SPILL COATED THIS AFRICAN PENGUIN—AND HUNDREDS OF OTHERS—WITH OIL. VOLUNTEER EFFORTS HAVE SAVED MANY PENGUINS HARMED BY ENVIRONMENTAL DISASTERS, BUT SOME DISASTERS OCCUR FAR OUT OF REACH OF HELP.

stable, penguin populations probably did so as well. Things changed, however, when the long European voyages of world exploration began in the sixteenth century.

For European explorers and sailors on those long voyages, often into unknown waters, the first question to ask about any new kind of wildlife was generally, "Can we eat it?" Almost always short of provisions, sometimes desperately so, seafaring adventurers regarded penguin colonies as meat markets. Some believed that God had placed the colonies along certain sailing routes—such as on islands at the southern tips of Africa and South America—especially to provide them with food. Many crews seeking penguins for their cook pots visited Isla Magdalena, in the Strait of Magellan, South Africa. The island used to be called Penguin Island for the large numbers of Magellanic penguins that nested there.

English explorer Sir Francis Drake landed on Penguin Island in 1575 and reported that "in the space of one day we killed no lesse than 3000" of the birds. Another English adventurer, Richard Hawkins, wrote a detailed description of a penguin hunt that took place in 1594. Hawkins described the hunt as "a great recreation to my company." His men armed themselves with clubs and formed a circle, driving the penguins to the center. If a penguin tried to break out, wrote Hawkins, "then was the sport." The men clustered the penguins together and clubbed their heads, killing at least a thousand at a time. They then split and washed the carcasses and preserved them in salt—sailors had discovered that salted penguin meat could be kept for up to two months and was a substitute for beef.

Many such accounts appear in the annals of early exploration, with staggering numbers of penguins killed. Even in more recent times, travelers have turned to penguins as a source of meat. Antarctic explorers relied on penguins for protein, and their journals describe a variety of cooking methods. Russian explorer Fabian von Bellingshausen, who visited Antarctica in 1819, wrote, "We had [penguin] stewed together with salt beef and gruel and seasoned with vinegar; the crew liked it. . . ." British explorer James Clark Ross, however, complained in 1841 that penguin meat had "a rank fishy flavour." Edward Wilson, who made several voyages to Antarctica with British explorer Robert Falcon Scott, wrote, "I could live indefinitely on [penguin] meat, and the eggs are most delicious. . . ." Wilson reported that the liver and half the breast of an emperor penguin made "a substantial meal for 16 men with nothing else but some peas, cocoa, and biscuit. We fried it in butter and it was excellent." A Swedish expedition led by Otto Nordensjköld in 1901–1902 spent a winter on an island off the coast of the Antarctic Peninsula. Penguin featured largely in their diet, as shown by excerpts from a single week's meal list: "breast of penguin and dried vegetables . . . salted penguin and beans . . . salted penguin . . . penguin and macaroni or rice . . . pastry and cold penguin . . . sardines and cold penguin." And Roald Amundsen of Norway, who led the first expedition to reach the South Pole and return safely, noted in one of his journals, "An emperor penguin just come on a visit—soup-kettle."

In some places, such as the Falkland Islands and Dassen Island off the South African coast, egging—the gathering of penguin eggs for food—was traditional until recent years. According to some reports, as many as half a million eggs were taken from Dassen Island each year during the 1920s. Laws passed since the 1960s have banned egging in most places, and although egging continues illegally, it is on a much smaller scale than before.

Penguins have provided people with more than just food. During the nineteenth and early twentieth centuries, some of the whaling and sealing crews that hunted in the southern seas also captured penguins for their skins or for the oil that could be boiled out of their fat. And on Macquarie Island, in 1891, a New Zealand businessman began boiling down penguins in huge iron kettles called digesters—a business that continued for a quarter of a century and killed as many as 150,000 penguins a year. Fortunately for the penguins, their oil never became a big business, and the twentieth-century commercial development of petroleum ended the exploitation of penguins and other sea creatures for oil. Ironically, though, the petroleum industry is one of the biggest perils penguins face in the modern world.

Modern Perils

Although penguins are protected by law everywhere they live, people still hunt them. In addition to illegal egging, fishermen in Africa, South America, and the subantarctic islands sometimes kill penguins for use as bait. The number of penguins destroyed in this way is small, however, compared with those that perish from other causes. Today, starving sailors with clubs aren't the biggest threat to penguins. Human activities that affect penguins indirectly are. Most people would agree that they don't *want* to harm penguins—but penguins are harmed by things people do for other reasons.

Shipping oil around the world in tankers and supertankers poses a major danger to penguins, and to countless other forms of marine life as well. Two of the world's major shipping routes pass through the waters around Cape Horn, at the southern tip of South America, and the Cape of Good Hope, at the southern tip of Africa. Both southern South America and southern Africa are home to penguins that feed in offshore waters and nest on beaches and offshore islands. Because of their large volume of shipping and their frequently rough seas, both regions are highly

A SIGN IN SIMONSTOWN, SOUTH AFRICA, WARNS MOTORISTS TO WATCH FOR PENGUINS. TRAFFIC CAN BE HAZARDOUS FOR THE BIRDS IN PLACES WHERE ROADS HAVE BEEN BUILT BETWEEN THE OCEAN AND TRADITIONAL NEST SITES.

vulnerable to accidents that could result in oil spills, possibly devastating to their penguin populations.

A 1968 spill off South Africa killed an estimated 15,000 African penguins. In 2000 the *Treasure*, a ship carrying iron ore, sank off South Africa, leaking 1,300 gallons of fuel oil into the

THE AFRICAN PENGUIN IS ONE OF SEVERAL SPECIES THAT HAS LONG LIVED CLOSE TO PEOPLE, AS ON THIS SOUTH AFRICAN BEACH.

sea. Although the amount of the spill was small, its location made it very dangerous—it was close to Dassen Island and Robben Island, two of the biggest African penguin colonies. In South America, Magellanic and Humboldt penguins face similar peril from spills. According to some estimates, as many as 40,000 Magellanic penguins die from oil pollution every year. Some wildlife experts, however, believe that an even greater danger to these species is oil pollution from everyday shipping activities in South American waters, where many vessels empty their ballast tanks. These tanks are filled with water to keep ships balanced, but they also contain signficant amounts of oil, gas, and other pollutants. When the tanks are emptied, the pollutants swirl into the sea along with the ballast water.

Every penguin population is at risk from oil spills. In 2001 a spill in the Galápagos Islands threatened the equatorial penguins there—until winds and currents carried the spill away from the penguin colonies. Even the once pristine Antarctic continent is not safe from oil spills. In 1989 an Argentine cruise ship ran aground near the Palmer Peninsula and spilled more than 150,000 gallons of fuel oil into the sea. Oil has also leaked into Antarctic waters from a Peruvian research vessel, from an American supply tanker, and from a variety of other ships. Such incidents place penguins at high risk, both in the open sea and on land, when oil washes onto beaches. Oil on penguins can blind them or injure their eyes, and it destroys the natural lubrication of their feathers. The greatest hazard, however, comes when oiled penguins try to clean themselves by preening. They swallow oil, which is often fatal.

Human activities other than shipping are also having significant effects on penguins. In some places, such as New Zealand, Australia, South Africa, and South America, penguins and people share the same real estate. The growth in human populations brings new roads, beach houses, malls, farms, and other developments, some of which destroy penguin habitat or interfere with penguins' lives. In some places in Australia, for example, little blue penguins have had to cross roads to get from the sea to their nests, although in most cases people have taken action to protect the penguins by rerouting the roads, establishing safe crossings, or acting as "traffic cops" during the penguins' hours of travel. And in some places where human development and activity have destroyed penguin habitat, individuals and local groups are now taking steps to encourage penguins to nest and to protect them.

People have introduced new predators to penguin environments. Where people go, animals such as rats, cats, dogs, and pigs also go. People have also introduced stoats and ferrets, members of the weasel family, to New Zealand. The effect of these introduced animals is especially devastating on islands that had no land-based predators, or few of them. Although rats, weasels, and cats cannot usually kill full-grown penguins, they raid nests, devouring eggs and chicks. Dogs have been known to kill adult birds.

Small wooden ships full of hungry sailors once preyed on penguins. Today, immense industrial fishing vessels called factory ships crisscross the southern oceans, so rich in life, harvesting great numbers of fish and shrimp. A few countries are even experimenting with harvesting krill and processing it into animal food or even food for people. These large-scale fishing operations threaten penguins in two ways. First, some penguins are caught and killed in nets or on long hooked lines. The second threat, though, is potentially much larger. Some wildlife experts fear that if people continue to harvest ever more food from the sea, the food supplies of penguins and other marine birds and mammals will shrink. Increased rates of hunger, disease, and starvation could bring about a decline in penguin populations because of human overfishing.

A final threat to penguins—as well as to many other life forms on land and in the sea—is global warming. Although scientists do not agree about the exact causes of global warming, most agree that it is taking place. According to an article published in the scientific journal *Nature* in May 2001, temperatures on the Antarctic Peninsula have risen about 2.5 degrees Fahrenheit (1.4 degrees Celsius) over the past fifty years. And over the past century, a quarter of Antarctica's sea ice has disappeared. These changes appear to have affected emperor, Adélie, and chinstrap penguins dramatically during the 1970s, when the size of many colonies decreased. The decline has stopped, and some populations even seem to be increasing, but some scientists fear that continued warming will result in more losses of penguin populations. Whether the cause of global warming is human pollution, a natural climate cycle, or both, its results could be deadly for penguins adapted to extreme cold.

Conservation

The size and stability of penguin populations vary greatly from species to species and from colony to colony. Macaronis, for example, have a total population of twelve million pairs or so. In sharp contrast are their relatives the royals, which breed only on Macquarie Island and which number about 850,000 pairs. The rarest penguin is probably the Galápagos, with fewer than 1,500 breeding pairs remaining.

The International Union for the Conservation of Nature and Natural Resources (IUCN), which organizes and oversees the activities of thousands of private and government conservation groups around the world, maintains a Penguin Conservation Assessment

and Management Plan (CAMP) to promote penguin protection. CAMP gives each species a status, from endangered to lower risk. The status of a species is based not just upon the number of surviving animals but also upon other factors, including the size of its range and threats to its habitat. According to the population studies and estimates that the IUCN uses, two species of penguins, the erect-crested (estimated at 200,000 pairs) and the Galápagos, are endangered. The IUCN regards a subspecies of the little blue penguin as a separate species. Known as the white-flippered penguin of New Zealand, it too is endangered.

The status just below endangered is vulnerable. CAMP ranks nine kinds of penguins as vulnerable. They are the Snares (23,000 pairs), Fiordland (from 1,000 to 5,000 pairs), royal, yellow-eyed (5,000 individuals), African (50,000 to 150,000 pairs), Humboldt (10,000 or more pairs), and three regional subspecies of rockhopper. The macaroni and Magellanic (more than a million pairs) penguins occupy the next danger level, with a classification of near threatened. At the lower risk status are the emperor, king, Adélie, chinstrap, gentoo, and little blue penguins.

Since the late twentieth century the world's southern oceans and its southernmost continent, Antarctica, have seen the rise of a new industry: tourism. Most people see penguins only in zoos, but an increasing number of travelers are venturing into the penguins' world to see these birds in their native habitats. The rise in tourism poses dangers, including a higher risk of marine accidents and oil spills and the possible disturbance of penguin colonies by overeager tourists. Most visits to

A BIOLOGIST INVESTIGATES A COLONY OF MACARONI PENGUINS ON SOUTH GEORGIA ISLAND, NEAR ANTARCTICA.

penguin colonies, however, are highly regulated by guides who know the rules and have an interest in protecting the penguins. Many experts feel that tourism can help penguins if it is carried out responsibly, includes education, and encourages travelers to support conservation. George Gaylord Simpson and Bernard Stonehouse, both of whom spent years studying penguins and made huge contributions to our knowledge of these flightless birds, both felt that penguins could benefit from careful tourism, just as they benefit from the careful management of penguin populations in zoos and marine-wildlife centers. People who enjoy penguins in such places are likely to learn something about them and their lives. They may also go on to promote penguin conservation with their votes or contributions.

The future of penguins depends upon many factors. Some, such as the warming of the earth's ocean and atmosphere, may be at least partly beyond human control. But many of the other factors that affect penguins, from overfishing to pollution, are human problems that people can correct if enough of them wish to do so. In the end, the survival of penguins—and of most other forms of wildlife on this planet—will depend upon human goodwill.

Goodwill *does* exist. Just ask any of the many volunteers who struggled to save African penguins smeared with oil after the sinking of the *Treasure* off South Africa in the year 2000. People hurried to Dassen Island and Robben Island. There, supervised by members of local conservation groups, they endured bites and blows from frightened penguins as they gathered the oiled birds and put them into boxes for transport to the mainland. More than 20,000 penguins were caught and ferried to the mainland, three to a box. When it appeared that another part of the oil spill was headed for Dassen Island, observers feared that the 22,000 birds that had not yet been oiled might be

The environment of the Falkland Islands has proved hospitable to people and their livestock as well as to penguins. Some of the first detailed studies and films of penguins were made in the Falklands.

hit next. Volunteers returned to the island and collected those birds. The treatment center on the mainland was full, so the unoiled penguins were carefully loaded onto livestock trucks and driven 500 miles (800 km) up the coast. They were released and immediately began swimming for home. Pollution-control authorities and volunteers worked frantically on Dassen Island to remove the oil. They managed to finish cleaning the colony just as the first of the long-distance swimmers returned to their home waters.

Meanwhile, workers at the cleaning station—helped by experts who flew in from around the world—cleaned and fed the oiled birds. Each bird had to be cleaned at least twice, and a vet examined each one before it was released. The whole process took several weeks. Volunteers fed and cared for the birds throughout this time. Then they ferried the penguins, one hundred or so at a time, to beaches for release. Tourists and sightseers, invited to help, carried boxes of penguins to the water's edge and watched as the penguins waddled together into groups, entered the sea, and struck out for their home islands. This dedicated, cooperative effort by thousands of people who worked to save oiled penguins would undoubtedly have astonished Richard Hawkins, whose men gathered to slaughter penguins, or the New Zealand businessman who boiled millions

of the birds for oil. Encouragingly, the *Treasure* spill workers managed to save 90 percent of the oiled penguins, a very high success rate for such efforts. Their success shows that—with goodwill, knowledge, and effort, people can keep penguins swimming through the southern seas for a long time to come.

Glossary

ancestral—having to do with ancestors or early forms

Antarctic Convergence—zone where cold Antarctic seawater meets warmer ocean currents, located worldwide at a latitude of about 50 degrees south of the Equator

extinct—no longer in existence

habitat—environment in which an animal lives; includes physical climate, type of landscape, prey, and predators

incubate—to keep an egg warm before the chick hatches

marine—having to do with the ocean

Northern Hemisphere—the half of the world north of the Equator

ornithologist—scientist who studies birds

paleontologist—scientist who studies extinct plants and animals, usually through fossils

pelagic—having to do with deep waters or the open ocean; oceangoing

Southern Hemisphere—the half of the world south of the Equator

spheniscine—having to do with penguins, members of the family Spheniscidae

subantarctic—located just north of or close to the Antarctic Circle

zoologist—scientist who studies animals

Species Checklist

Most zoologists and ornithologists recognize the seventeen species of penguins listed here.

Common Name	Scientific Name	Range
Emperor	*Aptenodytes forsteri*	Antarctica
King	*Aptenodytes patagonicus*	Subantarctic islands
Adélie	*Pygoscelis adeliae*	Antarctica
Chinstrap	*Pygoscelis antarctica*	Antarctic and subantarctic islands
Gentoo	*Pygoscelis papua*	Subantarctic islands
Rockhopper	*Eudyptes chrysocome*	Subantarctic islands
Macaroni	*Eudyptes chrysolophus*	Subantarctic islands: Atlantic, Indian oceans
Royal	*Eudyptes schlegeli*	Macquarie Island, south of Australia
Erect-crested	*Eudyptes sclateri*	Subantartic islands near New Zealand
Snares	*Eudyptes robustus*	Snares Island, New Zealand
Fiordland	*Eudyptes pachyrhynchus*	New Zealand
African*	*Spheniscus demersus*	Southern coast of South Africa
Humboldt**	*Spheniscus humboldti*	Coast of Peru, South America
Magellanic	*Spheniscus magellanicus*	South American coast, Falkland Islands
Galápagos	*Spheniscus mendiculus*	Galápagos Islands
Yellow-eyed	*Megadyptes antipodes*	New Zealand
Little blue***	*Eudyptula minor*	Australia, New Zealand, South Atlantic islands

*Also known as the black-footed or jackass penguin
**Also known as the Peruvian penguin
***Also known as the fairy penguin

Further Research

Books for Young People

Jango-Cohen, Judith. *Penguins*. New York: Benchmark Books, 2002.

Lynch, Wayne. *Penguins!* Buffalo, NY: Firefly Books, 1999.

Patent, Dorothy Hinshaw. *Looking at Penguins*. New York: Holiday House, 1993.

Reid, Keith. *Penguin*. Austin, TX: Raintree Steck-Vaughn, 2001.

Schlein, Miriam. *What's a Penguin Doing in a Place Like This?* Brookfield, CT: Millbrook Press, 1997.

Stefoff, Rebecca. *Penguin*. New York: Benchmark Books, 1998.

Stonehouse, Bernard. *Penguins: A Visual Introduction to Penguins*. New York: Checkmark, 1999.

Webb, Sophie. *My Season with Penguins: An Antarctic Journal*. New York: Houghton Mifflin, 2000.

Videos

Antarctic Wildlife. National Geographic Society, 1990.

Emperors of Antarctica. Discovery Communication, 1998.

Undersea World of Jacques Cousteau: Flight of Penguins. Pacific Arts Video, 1989.

World of Penguins. Educational Broadcasting Co., 2000.

Web Sites

www.pbs.org/wnet/nature/penguins
> The producers of the PBS series *Nature* maintain The World of Penguins, a site that features information, resources for further study, and links to other Web sites.

www.adelie.pwp.blueyonder.co.uk/
> Pete and Barb's Penguin Pages is one of the best and most informative Web sites on penguins, with hundreds of photos, more than a hundred pages of information on everything from species identification to evolution, and links to many other sites.

www.kidzone.ws/animals/penguins/
> This kid-friendly site offers a simple menu of penguin facts and photos.

www.penguins.cl
> The home page of the International Penguin Conservation Working Group, based in the Falkland Islands, contains information about worldwide threats to penguins and conservation efforts, as well as links to other conservation pages.

Bibliography

These books were especially useful to the author in researching this volume.

Ashworth, William and Art Wolfe. *Penguins, Puffins, and Auks: Their Lives and Behavior*. New York: Crown, 1993.

Chester, Jonathan. *The World of the Penguin*. San Francisco: Sierra Club Books, 1996.

Gorman, James. *The Total Penguin*. New York: Prentice-Hall, 1990.

Lanting, Frans. *Penguin*. New York: Taschen, 1999.

Marion, Remy. *Penguins: A Worldwide Guide*. New York: Sterling, 1999.

Naveen, Ron. *Waiting to Fly: My Escapades with the Penguins of Antarctica*. New York: Morrow, 1999.

Peterson, Roger Tory. *Penguins*. New York: Houghton Mifflin, 1975.

Reilly, Pauline. *Penguins of the World*. Oxford, England: Oxford University Press, 1994.

Schaefer, Kevin. *Penguin Planet*. Minnetonka, MN: NorthWord Press, 2000.

Stonehouse, Bernard. *The Biology of Penguins*. Baltimore: University Park Press, 1975.

Williams, Tony D. *The Penguins: Spheniscidae*. New York: Oxford University Press, 1995.

Index

Page numbers in **boldface** are illustrations.

About the Author

REBECCA STEFOFF is the author of many books for young readers about animals, nature, and evolution. Her previous contributions to the AnimalWays series include *Horses*, winner of the ASPCA Henry Bergh Children's Book Honor (2001). Stefoff also wrote *Penguins*, for very young readers, for Marshall Cavendish/Benchmark's The Science of Living Things series. She is a devoted bird-watcher who has not yet been privileged to see penguins in the wild but hopes to do so someday. For a list of her books, visit her Web site at www.rebeccastefoff.com.